ISBN 978-0-259-21343-7
PIBN 10738712

1 MONTH OF
FREE
READING

at

www.ForgottenBooks.com

By purchasing this book you are eligible for one month membership to ForgottenBooks.com, giving you unlimited access to our entire collection of over 700,000 titles via our web site and mobile apps.

To claim your free month visit:

www.forgottenbooks.com/free738712

English
Français
Deutsche
Italiano
Español
Português

www.forgottenbooks.com

Mythology Photography **Fiction**
Fishing Christianity **Art** Cooking
Essays Buddhism Freemasonry
Medicine **Biology** Music **Ancient
Egypt** Evolution Carpentry Physics
Dance Geology **Mathematics** Fitness
Shakespeare **Folklore** Yoga Marketing
Confidence Immortality Biographies
Poetry **Psychology** Witchcraft
Electronics Chemistry History **Law**
Accounting **Philosophy** Anthropology
Alchemy Drama Quantum Mechanics
Atheism Sexual Health **Ancient History**
Entrepreneurship Languages Sport
Paleontology Needlework Islam
Metaphysics Investment Archaeology
Parenting Statistics Criminology
Motivational

A

MOST SACRED CANTICLE

SE TO GOD THE CREATOR OF MAN,

WHO FOUNDED THE HEAVENS AND ALL THINGS THEREIN,

Is here given in Two Parts,

THE FIRST PART CONSISTS OF FIFTY-FOUR VERSES, AS FOLLOWS:

A Canticle of Praise on the Call of Abraham. .
A Canticle of Praise on the Exaltation of Joseph.
The Lost One meeting of the brethren.
A Canticle of Praise on Israel's going forth to Egypt.
A Canticle of Praise on the Deliverance of Israel from Bondage, and their wonderful preservation through the Red Sea and in the Desert.
Israel's established forever on the great Mount Sinai,

THE SECOND PART CONSISTS OF SIXTY-SIX VERSES, AS FOLLOWS;

A SACRED CANTICLE

OF PRAISE TO GOD AND OF HIM WHOM HE SENDS.

The Desired of Nations, of whose empire there's no end.

A Sacred Canticle of Praise to God who sent forth the Messiah Christ his only Son, and of his kingdom the Church.
A Sacred Canticle of Praise to our Lord and Saviour Jesus Christ, his Agony and Passion Crucifixion Death, and glorious Resurrection, his Ascension into heaven.
A Sacred Canticle of Praise to God on the Danger of Impiety, for which Nations have fell from the Church of thy judgment, Sins of Omission, voice of the Lamb.

PUBLISHED BY

PATRICK EDMOND O'SLEAUVEA,

No. 367 WAUBANSIA AVENUE, CHICAGO.

1872.

A
MOST SACRED CANTICLE

OF PRAISE TO GOD THE CREATOR OF MAN,

WHO FOUNDED THE HEAVENS AND ALL THINGS THEREIN,

Is here given in Two Parts,

THE FIRST PART CONSISTS OF FIFTY-FOUR VERSES, AS FOLLOWS:

A Canticle of Praise on the Call of Abraham.
A Canticle of Praise on the Exaltation of Joseph.
The Lost One meeting of the brethren.
A Canticle of Praise on Israel's going forth to Egypt.
A Canticle of Praise on the Deliverance of Israel from Bondage, and their wonderful preservation through the Red Sea and in the Desert.
Israel's established forever on the great Mount Sinai,

THE SECOND PART CONSISTS OF SIXTY-SIX VERSES, AS FOLLOWS:

A SACRED CANTICLE

OF PRAISE TO GOD AND OF HIM WHOM HE SENDS.

The Desired of Nations, of whose empire there's no end.

A Sacred Canticle of Praise to God who sent forth the Messiah Christ his only Son, and of his kingdom the Church.

A Sacred Canticle of Praise to our Lord and Saviour Jesus Christ, his Agony and Passion Crucifixion Death, and glorious Resurrection, his Ascension into heaven.

A Sacred Canticle of Praise to God on the Danger of Impiety, for which Nations have fell from the Church of thy judgment, Sins of Omission, voice of the Lamb.

PUBLISHED BY

PATRICK EDMOND O'SLEAUVEA,

No. 367 Waubansia Avenue, Chicago.

1872.

INTRODUCTION.

The Author of the following verses is well aware of not being able to do full justice to a subject of such vital importance to mankind, the Salvation of our Souls, as we have not occupied more than four lines of our limited space on any one topic connected with this most sacred subject, yet hath endeavored to give in a concise form an explicit view of the different parts connected with this most sublime subject, and it is given strictly according to the scriptural records of the Old and New Testament. These few verses are strong, plain and conclusive.

TO THE READER.

Dearly beloved, who read, peruse, or sing the following verses, if we have been of any assistance in bringing to your memory the sacred truths contained in these few lines, even then our hopes are somewhat realized; but if any of the truths contained in these few verses be of any assistance in impressing on your mind the necessity of leading a truly Christian life, then is our most fondest hope realized indeed.

Under the care of our good angel and protection of the Holy Mother of God, we this day dedicate this little work to our Lord Christ the Messiah, the Lamb, hoping that you who read these few lines, will be mindful of us in your prayer to God. We beg to be excused for all poetical or grammatical errors that may be found in these few verses, as we have given more preference to sacred truth.

> Praise the Lord, O ye Temple built under Darius,
> It shall be made more great than any former one,
> The orient from on high will glor'fy it in person,
> The Desired of Nations in't shall instruct thee, O man.

Entered according to Act of Congress, in the year 1872, by
PATRICK EDMOND O'SLEAUVEA,
In the Office of the Librarian of Congress, at Washington, D. C.

A

SACRED CANTICLE

OF PRAISE TO THE MOST HIGH GOD,

THE GREAT CREATOR OF MAN AND OF THE DELUGE.

———————

Praise ye the Lord thy God, who founded the heavens,
Planets, worlds, fill the regions of his endless domain,
Number'd, survey'd, yet beyond human conception,
Their grand order records the great glory of his name.
Praise the Lord, ye endless planetary regions,
Whose swift evolution by centrifugal force run,
Those great majestic work the terrestrial creation
Proclaims the unbound'd power of God, creator of man.

Praise ye the Lord, whose throne of glory's the heavens,
Great God Almighty, Eternal Creator of man,
Prince Eternal, peace great corner stone of glory,
Luminating great light heavens eternal Son.
Praise the Lord the most august holy Trinity,
Three persons in unison, Father, Spirit and Son,
One eternal, great undivided Divinity,
Whose great reign's glorified by his works angels and men.

Praise ye the Lord, thy great Eternal Creator,
Who hath given us life and existence his own;
Formed us of earth in his own spiritual likeness,
Partakers of his glory, heirs of his heavenly home.
Praise ye the Lord, O ye descendants of Adam,
Whose disobedience brought death, the wages of sin:
Thy son Cain went forth in his own self sufficieny,
Sought not the Lord, source of our strength, true wisdom
    in him.

Praise the Lord, O ye daughters of Eve, our mother,
When low in our fallen state, disobedience and sin,
He said, Woman's seed would crush the serpent forever,
By the blood of his beloved eternal son.
Praise the Lord, ye holy patriarch's from Adam,
Who walked in his holy way, taught by his word;
Enoch's found blameless, he's translated into heaven,
From midst man's sinful disobedience to the Lord.

Praise ye the Lord, O ye decendants of Noah,
Who only was found ritious in sight of his God;
He building the Ark, according to the pattern,
By faith saved his generation, man, from the flood.
Praise the Lord, ye numerous offspring of Noah,
Ever remember that scourge devastating flood,
For man's wicked crimes, sin and dreadful disobedience,
He o'erwhelm'd the earth and sinful man in the flood.

A

SACRED CANTICLE

OF GREAT PRAISE TO GOD,

ON THE CALL, OF ABRAHAM FROM AMIDST THE CHALDEAN AND OF ISRAEL.

———◆———

Praise ye the Lord, ye descendants of Abraham,
Whom he hath call'd forth from amidst the Chaldean,
Promised in his seed all nations would be bless'd,
And make of him a Nation in his faith to teach man.
Praise ye the Lord, whose Love for mankind's forever,
Great the mighty promises he made to Abraham,
All Land from Egypt to the great river Euphrates,
The Dominion of Israel, th' holy lands of Canaan.

Praise ye the Lord, ye descendants of Israel,
In your envy, malice, wicked devices, your own,
Sold your belov'd brother Joseph to foreign bondage,
Banish'd him forever from his father's blest home.
Praise ye the Lord, our most merciful Father,
Who was with him through strange lands to Joseph
    unknown,
Gave unto him the great spirit of revelation;
He interpreting Pharaoh's dreams of great famine to come.

Praise ye the Lord, whose Spirit exalted joseph,
His intregrity of soul, 'tis this day made known,
Pharaoh discerning Joseph's great spirit of wisdom,
Proclaim'd him Governor of Egypt o'er his great home.
Praise ye the Lord, whose mercy endureth forever,
Seven years of great plenty o'er Egypt hath come,
Fill'ng her vast stores, gran'ries increased beyond number,
With grain purchas'd by Pharaoh for th' great famine to
    come.

Praise the Lord, whose decrees are fulfill'd forever,
Seven years great famine o'er Egypt and borders is sent,
Throughout all Canaan beyond the great River Jordan,
Great famine prevailing, want of food and corn is felt.
Praise the Lord, two years and yet famine more prevailing,
Great scarcity is felt throughout the Lands of Canaan,
Israel's sons are gone forth to Egypt to buy corn,
To provide for their Father's great household and home.

Praise the Lord, most just and merciful, forever,
They're strangers, must apply to the governor alone,
Joseph perceives they are his own beloved brethren.
Said by Pharaoh, your're spies, for invasion hath come.
Praise be the Lord, we're not spies, but twelve sons of one
    father,
One's dead, the other remains with his father at home,
We are peaceable men, and come forth to buy corn,
Great famine prevailing, in Canaan there is none.

Praise the Lord, they are forthwith cast into prison,
Charged with being spies against Pharaoh's great throne;
Three days they await the decision of Pharaoh,
Shut in prison they weep for crimes 'gainst Joseph they've
    done.
Praise be the Lord, they are called forth from prison,
The decision of Pharaoh to them is made known;
Simon must remain yet a hostage, with Pharaoh,
Whilst the rest may return with grain for father's great
    home.

Praise ye the Lord, they arrived with corn from Egypt,
Their whole case herein stated, to their father made known,
They were imprison'd as spies, Simon detained a hostage,
Till they bring their youngest brother Benjamin from home.
Praised be the Lord, said Israel, as he bow'd weeping,
Joseph, he's dead you told me, by wild beasts was slain,
Simon remains yet a hostage with Pharoah;
Mishap befalls Benjamin, I'll go mourning to my grave.

Praise the Lord, Israel's sons again gone forth to Egypt,
Benjamin they present before governor and king,
Simon, he's released from prison as a hostage,
Presently he's brought forth and deliver'd unto them.
Praise ye the Lord, whose spirit dwelleth in Joseph,
His great heart fill'd with true benevolence most kind,
Sons of Israel accept th' Governor's hospitality,
Twelve sons of Israel this night in his mansion shall dine.

A
SACRED CANTICLE
OF PRAISE TO GOD ON JOSEPH'S PROSPERITY,
THE LOST ONE, MEETING OF THE BRETHREN.

Praise ye the Lord, they are gone forth to the mansion,
Where dinner's prepared, name, age, rank, marks their seat,
They'r received with great joy by the Governor at table,
Dividends of honor'd birth comes forth on each plate.
Praise be the Lord, your aged Father yet liveth,
I presume he's a man of year's advanc'd in age,
If you'd know how I love to look on his features,
Seems he must be of honor'd birth and great parentage.

Praised be the Lord, Israel our Father yet liveth,
He's of Isaac, his mother Rachel, Melcha's race,
His grandsire's, Abraham called forth from the Chaldean,
Of Sem, descendant of Seth, that patriarchal sage.
Praised be the Lord, at this veiled grand reception,
The great designs of the Most High is'nt none to man,
This shall be a proverb 'ere' spoken by the nation's
Toast, Let all mankind come, there's corn in Egypt for them.

Praised be the Lord, Simon released from prison,
They on their way rejoice, their reception's most kind,
Lo, a courier is dispatch'd, order'd to detain them,
Charged with taking master's cup, he's wont to divine.
Praised be the Lord, such a crime charged against Israel,
They're then brought back before the Governor arraign'd,
Search made the cup's found in the sack of Benjamin,
The rest are all liberated while Benjamin's detained.

Praise ye the Lord, Israel's sons sore, sore they're weeping,
They would rather perish than return without Benjamin.
All said, we'll become master's bond slaves forever,
Let the boy return to his aged Father in Canaan.
Praised be the Lord, Joseph longer can't restrain himself,
Cried aloud, his tears gushing forth like torrents they flow,
Draw you near unto me that I may embrace you,
I am Joseph, your brother to foreign bondage you sold.

Praise the Lord, Israel's sons in great joy they're weeping,
Loud, loud, they cried, their tears of affection doth flow,
Lost one is found, dead's yet living, Joseph whom they sold,
Before him in joy'd sorrow'ng contrition they bow.
Praise ye the Lord, Israel's cry is heard at a distance,
Their mingled tears of joy long continues to flow,
They wept, they have cried nigh like to distraction,
Fully satisfied, their tears gently cease to flow.

Praised be the Lord, said Joseph unto his brethren.
Be not angry concerning what you've done unto me,
'Twas the will of the Lord I came here before you,
To have a place prepared that I might preserve thee.
Praised be the Lord, Israel, my father, yet liveth,
Tell him Joseph's living and of my great prosperity,
Let Israel, my father, come forth and sojourn in Egypt,
The lands of Goshen he'll dwell and be nourish'd by me.

SACRED CANTICLE

OF PRAISE TO GOD,

ON ISRAEL'S GOING FORTH TO EGYPT.

Praised be the Lord, Israel's gone forth to Egypt,
When that he came to the great well of the Oath,
He there alights for the night and sacrificed victims,
Renews his covenants to God by word and acts both.
Praise the Lord, who said, I'll go down with you to Egypt,
And make of thee a mighty great nation of men,
Again bring thee back and establish thee forever,
Give to thy posterity the holy lands of Canaan.

Praise the Lord, Israel's arrived with Joseph in Egypt,
In tears of affection oft each other embraced,
His face seem'd like the guardian angel of Israel,
Since Joseph yet lives, let thy servant depart in peace.
Praise the Lord, seventeen years Israel yet liveth
They're assembled, his last prophetic words to hear,
Behold the scepter shall not depart from Judah,
Till he comes the desired, him the nations shall hear.

Praise ye the Lord, many years and Joseph's not living,
Other Pharaoh's have arisen who know not the Lord,
Jealous of Israel's increasing prosperity,
Conspir'd to enslave by task masters press them to work.
Praise the Lord, who permitted Israel's captivity,
For four hundred years a mission in Egypt to man,
That their faith be impress'd on the bosom soul of mankind,
That there does exist a God that rules in the kingdom of
  man.

A

SACRED CANTICLE

OF PRAISE TO GOD,

FOR THE DELIVERANCE OF ISRAEL FROM BONDAGE IN THEIR WONDERFUL FLIGHT
THROUGH THE RED SEA.

Praise the Lord ye great deliverer's of Israel,
Moses and Aaron commission'd from on high,
To lead forth Israel from the house of bondage,
Pharoah persists to refuse Egypt's first born must die.
Praise the Lord who instituted the paschal festivity.
Commands Israel the paschal lamb to sacrifice,
Sprinkle with its blood door posts lintle of Israel,
Sign of man's redemption, when Egypt's first born must die.

Praise the Lord, Egypt's first born lies dead this morning,
Sore, sore they have wept, and loud, loud they cried,
Let Israel depart from our midst now and forever,
Pharaoh continues to refuse, all in Egypt must die.
Praised be the Lord, Israel is gone forth from Egypt,
From the house of bondage by the strong arm of the Lord,
Led forth to the desert by way of the Red Sea,
Pharaoh viewing them straighten'd, pursues with army and
    sword.

Praise ye the Lord, whose cloud shaded them from Pharaoh,
A bright pillar of fire direct their way by night,
When on the coast Moses commands the sea to open,
Israel's pass over by God saved in their flight.
Praise ye the Lord, Pharaoh's forces still pursuing,
Their whole force advancing as up on solid ground,
Moses strikes the sea, foaming billows returning,
O'erwhelmed is Pharaoh, Egypt's great force is drown'd.

Praise the Lord, magnify his great name forever,
Who upheld Israel's path across the foaming deep,
Whilst Pharaoh's pride, Egypt's force's engulft forever,
Those blood spilling warriors in the red sea they sleep.
Praise the Lord who dwelt in tabernacles with Israel,
In their thirst gave forth water from that typical rock,
He fed them with manna from the dews of heaven,
For their evening repast the quail came forth in flocks.

Praise ye the Lord, whose ordinance is forever,
He call'd Moses to come forth to the holy mount,
There he'd receive the holy commandments of Israel,
All Israel shall hear. Let them touch not the mount.
Praise ye the Lord, who appeared unto Moses,
Gave to him tablets the law on the great Mount Sinai,
That they might be the rule, guiding star of our actions,
Israel's established forever by the Lord God most high.

This glorious scene took place on the fifteenth day after the paschal solemnity.

A

SACRED CANTICLE

OF PRAISE TO THE LORD,

AND OF HIM WHOM HE SENDS, IN WHOSE EMPIRE THERE'S NO END OF PEACE.

———————•———————

Praise ye the Lord, and exalt His name forever,
Of Him whom he sends, the prophets in hallow'd words sing,
Israel's hope is our Lord, the desir'd of nations,
Christ the Messiah, high priest, the victim, their King.
Praise ye the Lord, our most holy Redeemer,
The Lord of Hosts, Israel's Creator, our King,
The Lord, He's become the Paschal Lamb, our atonement,
Ye heavens respond, His hallow'd praises we sing.

Praise th' Lord, by whom the Prophet Isaias hath spoken,
Said, therefore, the Lord will give unto thee a sign,
A Virgin shall conceive, bear her son Emmanuel,
Holy one of Israel, God, thy Redeemer Divine.
Prais'd be the Lord, a Child 's born to us of Mary,
A Son's given to us, begotten of the Most High,
Principalities resting upon His shoulders,
Wonderful Counselor, God the mighty is He.

Praise ye the Lord, O, Mary, belov'd Virgin Mother,
Of wonderful Counselor, God's Eternal Son,
He is our Advocate, justification forever,
Great God, the Mighty, Father of the world to come,
Praise the Lord who chose the blessed blest Virgin Mary,
Who brought forth our Redeemer, Israel's holy one,
Prince, eternal peace, Emmanuel, O, Jesus!
Who sent forth His Holy Church on earth to teach man.

Praise ye the Lord, beloved sacred spouse of the Father,
Who appear'd in heaven, her robes more bright than the sun,
Her crown is twelve stars, wreath'd in gems most radiant,
Heaven's glorious Queen, for her footpath the moon.
Prais'd be the Lord, she hath travail'd in child birth,
Brought forth Israel's King, Heaven's Eternal Son,
Whose great reign is peace, glorious, perpetual,
In Thy kingdom, the Church, mid the nations of men.

Praise ye the Lord, thou, O Bethlehem, sweet little one,
Out of thee shall He come, Israel's great King, our Lord,
His going forth 's from beyond the day star of eternity,
He is thy Creator, the great Eternal Word.
Praise the Lord, O ye habitation of Zion,
And greatly rejoice, ye virgin daughters of man,
From midst thee 's chosen Mary thy loved Virgin Mother,
Who brought forth, gave this world Christ, her redeeming
    Son.

Praise the Lord, whose Empire 's establish'd forever,
In His sacred dominion laws of justice ne'er cease,
Seated on His throne, to establish it forever,
He is the Lord of Hosts, Israel's great King of Peace.
Praise the Lord, whose dominion 's enlarg'd forever,
In thy glorious kingdom there's no end of peace,
His cherubic throne their wings stretched forth in mercy,
He's the Lord God most high, eternal Prince of Peace.

Praise ye the Lord, whose word Daniel hath spoken,
From Israel's gone forth to build the temple he told.
Yet seventy weeks and Christ their great King is slay'd,
Those who conspir'd His death shall not be of His fold.
Praise the Lord, whose word Malachies hath spoken,
From the rising of the sun, going forth of the same,
There sacrifice, and My name's great among the Gentiles,
A pure oblation shall be offered to my name.

Praise ye the Lord, the great Almighty Jehovah,
No one knoweth the Father but His belov'd Son,
Son's only known by the great Almighty Father,
Whose immensity's beyond the conception of man.
Praise ye the Lord, the most mighty, most holy,
Infinite, eternal, omnipotent, most high,
Whose unbound'd glory 's beyond conception of mortals,
Only finds equal glory mid the great Trinity.

SACRED CANTICLE

OF PRAISE TO OUR LORD, THE MOST HOLY MESSIAH,

AND OF HIS KINGDOM THE CHURCH.

Praise ye the Lord, exalt His great name forever,
Who sent forth the Messiah, Christ His only Son,
To establish His kingdom, peace with man forever,
The holy Church of Christ empower'd by the great I AM,
Praise ye the Lord, O holy Church of the Messiah,
Great City of the Lamb, the new Jerusalem,
Seen in vision by St. John descending from the Father,
Whose luminating great light, 's the Messiah, the Lamb.

Praise the Lord, ye chief Apostle chosen by Jesus,
Who found'd His holy Church, built on thee, Peter, a rock,
Hell or spirit of error shall not prevail against her,
Faithful Shepherd, said Jesus, feed my lambs, sheep and
    flock,
Praise the Lord, ye who's given the great keys of heaven,
Empower'd to make laws to guide His holy Church,
Said lo I am with you all days, even forever,
Sovereign, Pontiff, Chief, Guardian in Christ's Holy Church.

Praise the Lord, you Apostles chosen by Jesus,
Foundation gems His blood cemented on this rock,
Whose names are inscribed on its foundation forever,
True shepherds of Jesus, guarding His holy flock,
Praise the Lord, ye holy priests, disciples of Jesus,
Sent forth establishing His great kingdom of peace,
Teaching man to love. the Lord, walk in chaste obedience
Keep'ng the holy commandments of God and His Church.

Praise ye the Lord, you the chosen of Israel,
Jesus rebuilds His holy Church, New Jerusalem,
Corporat'd in the Father, inspir'd by the Holy Ghost,
And sealed by the blood of God's eternal Son.
Praise ye the Lord, O most holy Church of Jesus,
A monument bright, a mountain of light set on hills,
Watchmen on its towers, sentinels, ne'er cease still,
Shows the footprints of Jesus, His law, peace, love and
good will.

Praise ye the Lord, you true believers in Jesus,
Walk in His holy way, pious, firm, faithful and true,
Love His holy Church as thy true mother in Jesus,
Sent forth inspired by the Holy Ghost to teach you,
Praise the Lord, ye baptised, truly cleansed in Jesus;
Walk ye in His blest path, keep pure, holy from sin,
Your hearts and souls in great zeal to God dedicat'd,
Exemplified great lights, instructing fallen man.

Praise ye our Lord, who gave us His peace forever,
Thus 'tis His sacred peace which this world cannot give,
Peace within our souls, being subject to the spirit,
T'is this everlasting peace wherein ye shall live.
Praise ye the Lord, whose Church in Spirit empower'd,
To absolve those from sin who truly penitent came,
And give them to eat this living bread from heaven,
Their blest joyful festivity's Christ, the paschal lamb.

Praise ye the Lord, behold God is my Saviour,
Our faith, hope, life and strength, O, Lord, 'tis in thee,
Who gave us to eat this living bread from heaven,
Rejoice, ye, O man, thy God's enthroned in thee.
Praise ye the Lord, our most loving Saviour,
Who gave us to drink waters of life from above
Erecting in our souls ; the sweet fountain of Jesus
All he asks in return, keep His commandment of love.

Praise ye our Lord, the most holy Messiah,
Who establishd his kingdom 'mid the nations of man,
Whose glorious King's Christ, our high priest forever,
In the eternal council most high is Christ, the meek lamb
Praise the Lord, ye thrones, beware of National encroach-
    ments,
Covet not the vineyard planted by the great King,
Lest thy grasp, slay the Son heir of his inheritance,
O dreadful's th' scourge His avenging justice must bring.

SACRED CANTICLE

OF PRAISE TO OUR LORD.

AND SAVIOUR JESUS CHRIST, HIS PASSION, DEATH AND GLORIOUS RESURRECTION.

Praise ye the Lord, He's gone forth to Jerusalem,
He'll be rejected, condemn'd, scourged, crucified, slayed ;
Israel knows not the time of her great visitation,
Christ the Messiah, their King, meek Lamb, the betray'd.
Praise ye the Lord, who wept over Jerusalem ;
In one week the oblation of bullocks, rams, cease.
Christ, he is the paschal lamb of redemption, the
Ever atoning divine oblation of peace.

Praise ye the Lord you virgin daughters of Israel,
Thy King cometh forth riding meek, humble and poor,
He'd have built his holy church Jerusalem forever,
But they reject'd their Lord Israel, great King of the poor.
Praise the Lord who on that solemn paschal evening
A New Testament his blood in Israel solemnized,
Bequeath'd us His body, blood, soul and divinity,
Living bread Life of our Soul he for us sacrificed.

Praise ye the Lord, whose sorrow'ng prayer in the garden
Oppress'd Divine grief for man sin'd against his Lord,
Thrice pray'd Father, accept thy Son their victim, justice
Grieved, divine contrition, blood sweat por'd forth from
    our Lord.
Praise ye the Lord whose great internal wisdom
Guards approach, he's betray'd, Judas, low perfid's man,
He's led before Cephas, condemn'd by high priest and
    council,
Thrice by Peter denied, saying " I know not the man."

Praise ye the Lord Jesus, arraigned before Pilate,
Who declares he finds no fault worthy death in the man,
Takes water testimony before the nation.
I wash my hands from blood of this just, holy man.
Praise the Lord. The Jews cried aloud, crucify him,
Let his blood be upon us, our children and sons,
He hath assumed to be the great King of Israel,
Thou can'st be Cæsar's friend and permit this man to live.

Praise the Lord, the Jews threatens Pilate with Cæsar,
Whose favor he assents just holy one to sacrifice,
His sentence he writes, in Greek, Latin and Hebrew,
Jesus of Nazareth, King of the Jews, shall be crucified.
Praise the Lord, Christ as a lamb's led forth to the slaughter,
He's as one dumb, not open'g his mouth to reply,
In humble obedience he's gone forth to Calvary,
On his wounded shoulders the cross on which he's to die.

Praise the Lord, on his journey to Mount Calvary,
Through loss of blood, great weakness, thrice he falls to
    the ground,
Simon the Syrian 's compell'd to assist him,
Carry the cross, on with rough nails he's to be bound.
Praise ye the Lord, on Calvary's cross he's exalted,
His divine arms extended, resting on his wounds,
Three long hours on the cross in suffering affliction,
Praying " Father, forgive them, they know not what they do."

Praise ye the Lord, on Calvary's cross he expired.
His death consummated, great works of his love!
Humane, divine, united, eternal atonement,
Appeased God's great justice, restored man to his love.
Praise the Lord. Lower'd from the cross of his crucifixion,
And stretched on the bosom of his mother's love,
Whose anguish deep grieved sorrowing affliction,
Is wounded in compassion for death of her beloved son.

Praise the Lord, to the Valley of Death he's descended,
Bright rays of his wounds their great redemption proclaims,
Issues forth from heaven's Son long desired in Israel,
Who led forth those loved captives from death's gloomy
    chains.
Praise th' Lord ye just, I am thy glorious resurrection,
In me heaven's your own perpetual praise to sing,
I am the hope, life and strength of humane perfection,
The holy one of Israel thy creator your king.

Praise the Lord. The third day after his crucifixion,
Once more on earth he triumphant glorious appears,
Stood in the midst of the Apostles in piety,
They being assembl'd in prayer, doors shut with fear.
Praise the Lord. He said, peace be unto you forever,
Be ye not troubled, see here my wounds, it is I;
Look ye into my side, my hands, feet and shoulders,
As I told you before, I'd meet you in Galilee.

Prais'd be the Lord, he raised his hands and bless them,
All power's mine, in heaven and on this earth below;
As the living Father hath sent me forth unto you,
In his great holy power I send you also.
Praise ye the Lord, who raised his hands and breath'd on
    them,
Whose sins you forgive on earth they'r forgiven above,
Whose sins you retain they are retain'd in heaven,
Remain in this place till endow'd by th' spirit of Love.

Praise ye the Lord, Jesus ascends to the Father,
Paraclete the comforter he'd send from above,
Great Spirit of light to instruct them forever,
Their great guiding spirit, truth and heavenly love.
Praise the Lord, fiftieth day after his crucifixion,
Holy Ghost descends on the Apostles from above,
Spirit of truth to teach them all truth forever,
Abide with them all time their great Spirit of Love.

Praise ye the Lord God, our most beloved Father,
He sent forth the Messiah Christ his belov'd Son,
Who established his church, authorized forever,
The holy church of Christ empower'd to teach man.
Praise ye the Lord, in whose great eternal glory,
Holy Trinity Father, great Spirit and Son,
One eternal great undivided Divinity,
Hear ye O Israel, the Eternal is one.

A

SACRED CANTICLE

OF PRAISE TO THE MOST HIGH,

ON THE DANGER OF IMPIETY AND DISOBEDIENCE.

Praise ye the Lord, and exalt His name forever,
Great his mighty works and visitations he sent,
See Asia's vast plains overwhelmed in darkness,
Where the Apostles of Jesus his gospel did plant,
Praise ye the Lord and exalt his name forever,
Egypt where Christ's gospel preach'd by his belov'd John
Their lamps of light removed, dreadful darkness cover
Profigur'd words from Egypt, I've called forth my Son.

Praise ye the Lord and exalt his name forever,
See that vast empire city on th' Bosphorus built,
Whose dominion in Europe extend'd into Asia,
Fertile plains of Judea's fields where Christ's blood was spilt.
Praise ye the Lord and exalt his name forever,
Great his mighty works and visitations he sent,
For heresy, schism, sin and dreadful disobedience,
This vast empire overwhelm'd by th' false prophet the turk.

Praise ye the Lord, and look around Europe borders,
Many nations hurl'd forth accursed from his holy church,
For heresy, schism, sin, lust, incest and murder,
Blind wand'ring isms toil in vain to whelm Christ's holy
    church.
Praise the Lord, O man, and remember forever
Lukewarm Christians. your danger position is such,
Branch's not worthy life in the stem brambles to be burnt,
And hurl'd forever accursed from his holy church.

Praise the Lord, O man, be ye fervent and zealous,
Enter ye the straight gate by strict justice and right,
Broad and varied the vices lead to destruction,
Thy faith darken'd by sin oft yields but dim light.
Praise ye the Lord, and hear you his church forever,
Only authority on earth given to teach man,
Holy church of Christ pillar of truth forever,
Where fools cannot err whose heart dwells truly therein.

Praise the Lord O man, and remember thy judgment,
'Tis spoken by St. Paul, man's works by fire is tried,
If his works burns suffers loss purified by fire,
His works continue to burn dreadful death he's died.
Praise the Lord O man, beware th' sins of omission,
In works of true charity continually abide,
Thy soul may rejoice in the voice of the Lamb saying,
Come ye blest of my Father, with me his great glory enjoy.
Glory, honor and praise be to Thee, O Lord,
And may the most just, the most high and most amiable
Will of God be done, prais'd and exalted in all things
    forever.